THE LIBRARY OF CONTEMPORARY THOUGHT

*America's most original voices
tackle today's most provocative issues*

CARL HIAASEN

TEAM RODENT
*How Disney Devours
the World*

"Revulsion is good. Revulsion is healthy. Each of us has limits, unarticulated boundaries of taste and tolerance, and sometimes we forget where they are. Peep Land is here to remind us; a fixed compass point by which we can govern our private behavior. Because being grossed out is essential to the human experience; without a perceived depravity, we'd have nothing against which to gauge the advance or decline of culture—our art, our music, our cinema, our books. Without sleaze, the yardstick shrinks at both ends. Team Rodent doesn't believe in sleaze, however, nor in old-fashioned revulsion. Square in the middle is where it wants us all to be, dependable consumers with predictable attitudes. The message, never stated but avuncularly implied, is that America's values ought to reflect those of the Walt Disney Company, and not the other way around."

Also by Carl Hiaasen

Stormy Weather
Strip Tease
Native Tongue
Skin Tight
Double Whammy
Tourist Season
Lucky You

TEAM RODENT

How Disney Devours the World

CARL HIAASEN

THE LIBRARY OF CONTEMPORARY THOUGHT
THE BALLANTINE PUBLISHING GROUP • NEW YORK

The Library of Contemporary Thought
Published by The Ballantine Publishing Group

Copyright © 1998 by Carl Hiaasen

All rights reserved under International and Pan-American Copyright Conventions. Published in the United States by The Ballantine Publishing Group, a division of Random House, Inc., New York, and simultaneously in Canada by Random House of Canada Limited, Toronto.

http://www.randomhouse.com

Library of Congress Cataloging-in-Publication Data
Hiaasen, Carl.
Team rodent : how Disney devours the world /
Carl Hiaasen.—1st ed.
p.   cm. — (The library of contemporary thought)
ISBN 0-345-42280-5 (alk. paper)
1. Walt Disney Company.   I. Title.   II. Series.
PN1999.W27H53   1998
384'.8'0979494—dc21   98–16565
CIP

Text design by Holly Johnson
Cover design and illustration by Ruth Ross

Manufactured in the United States of America

First Edition: May 1998

10   9   8   7   6   5   4   3   2   1

Acknowledgments

For their assistance I am indebted to the intrepid
Liz Donovan and the daring Jennifer Dienst.

Ready to Drop

DATELINE: TIMES SQUARE, November 1997.
Deloused and revitalized Times Square,
home to MTV, Condé Nast, Morgan Stanley, the
world's biggest Marriott hotel, the Ford Center
for the Performing Arts, and soon a Madame Tus-
saud's wax museum.

And Peep Land. From its doorway on West
Forty-second Street one can see the glittering
marquee of the new Disney Store at Broadway.
More importantly, from the Disney Store one can
clearly see Peep Land: a scrofulous, neon-lit affir-
mation of XXX-rated raunch.

Sleaze lives.

It lives and it beckons, though less garishly
than either the Disney Store or its rococo neigh-
bor, the New Amsterdam Theater, where golden

breeze-furled banners advertise *The Lion King*, a musical based on a cartoon movie. Both the cartoon (which grossed $772 million worldwide) and the stage show (which will most likely be the most successful production in Broadway history) were created as exemplary family entertainment by the Walt Disney Company, which also lavishly restored the New Amsterdam at a cost of $38 million.

In this way Disney audaciously has set out to vanquish sleaze in its unholiest fountainhead, Times Square; the skanky oozepot to which every live sex show, jack-off arcade, and smut emporium in the free world owes its existence. For decades, city and state politicians had vowed to purge the place of its legendary seediness, in order to make the streets safe, clean, and attractive for out-of-town visitors. New Yorkers paid no attention to such fanciful promises, for Times Square was knowledgeably regarded as lost and unconquerable; a mephitic pit, so formidably infested that nothing short of a full-scale military occupation could tame it. As recently as 1994 Times Square swarmed unabashedly with hookers, hustlers, and crackheads and was the address of forty-seven porn shops.

Then Disney arrived, ultimate goodness versus

ultimate evil, and the cynics gradually went silent. Times Square has boomed.

The dissolute, sticky-shoed ambience of Forty-second Street has been subjugated by the gleamingly wholesome presence of the Disney Store. Truly it's a phenomenon, for the shelves offer nothing but the usual cross-merchandised crapola: snow globes, wristwatches, charm bracelets, figurines, and lots of overpriced clothes. Hard-core fans can buy matching Mickey and Minnie garden statues, a $400 Disney Villains chess set, or a twenty-fifth-anniversary Disney-edition Barbie doll, complete with teensy mouse ears. Your basic high-end tourist trap is what it is.

Yet somehow the building radiates like a shrine—because it's not just any old store, it's a *Disney* store, filled with *Disney* characters, Mickey and Minnie at play in the fields of Times Fucking Square. And evidently the mere emplacement of the iconic Disney logo above the sidewalks has been enough to demoralize and dislodge some of the area's most entrenched sin merchants.

The mayor of New York says that's a good thing, and citizens agree: good for tourism, good for children, good for the morale of the community. If Times Square can be redeemed, some would say, then no urban Gomorrah is beyond salvation. All you need is a Disney retail outlet! (As of this writing, there are more than 550 in eleven countries.)

It's not surprising that one company was able to change the face of Forty-second Street, because the same company changed the face of an entire state, Florida, where I live. Three decades after it began bulldozing the cow pastures and draining the marshes of rural Orlando, Disney stands as by far the most powerful private entity in Florida; it goes where it wants, does what it wants, gets what it wants. It's our exalted mother teat, and you can hear the sucking from Tallahassee all the way to Key West.

The worst damage isn't from the Walt Disney World Resort itself (which is undeniably clean, well operated, and relatively safe) or even from the tourists (although an annual stampede of forty million Griswolds cannot help but cut an untidy swath). The absolute worst thing Disney did was to change how people in Florida thought about money; nobody had ever dreamed there could be so much. Bankers, lawyers, real-estate salesmen, hoteliers, restaurateurs, farmers, citrus growers—everyone in Mickey's orb had to drastically recalibrate the concepts of growth, prosperity, and what was possible. Suddenly there were no limits. Merely by showing up, Disney had dignified blind greed in a state pioneered by undignified greedheads. Everything the company touched turned to gold, so everyone in Florida craved to touch or be touched by Disney. The gates opened, and in galloped fresh hordes. The cattle ranches, orange groves, and cypress stands of old Orlando rapidly gave way to an execrable panorama of suburban blight.

One of the great ironies upon visiting Disney World is the wave of relief that overwhelms you upon entering the place—relief to be free of the nerve-shattering traffic and the endless ugly sprawl. By contrast the Disney resort seems like a verdant sanctuary. That was the plan, of course—Team Rodent left the park buffered with thousands of unspoiled acres, to keep the charmless roadside schlock at bay.

As Orlando exploded, business leaders (and therefore politicians) throughout the rest of Florida watched and plotted with envy. Everyone conspired for a cut of the Disney action, meaning overflow. The trick was to catch the tourists after they departed the Magic Kingdom: induce them to rent a car and drive someplace else and spend what was left of their vacation money. This mad obsession for sloppy seconds has paid off big-time.

By the year 2000, the number of tourists visiting the Orlando area is expected to reach forty-six million annually. That's more than the combined populations of California and Pennsylvania storming into Florida every year, an onslaught few places on earth could withstand. Many Disney pilgrims do make time to search for auxiliary amusement in other parts of the state. High on the list is the southernmost chain of islands known as the Keys, where I live, and where only one road runs the length of the archipelago. Maybe you can appreciate my concern.

Disney's recent ambitions in Times Square are modest compared to its original mission in Florida: to establish a sovereign state within a state, a private entertainment mecca to which every working family in America would be lured at least once and preferably several times. And that's exactly what has come to pass. Disney World is the most-visited vacation destination on the planet; kids who went there in the 1970s are bringing their own kids today, perpetuating a brilliantly conceived cycle of acculturation. Every youngster who loves a Disney theme park—and almost all of them do—represents a potential lifetime consumer of all things Disney, from stuffed animals to sitcoms, from Broadway musicals to three-bedroom tract homes. With this strategy Disney will someday tap into the fortunes of every person on the planet, as it now does to every American whether we know it or not.

And though the agents of its takeover are omnipresent and not always identified, it's still unnerving to enter the non-Disney Virgin Megastore in Times Square and see Kathie Lee on the ultralarge TV screen. This would be Kathie Lee Gifford, the talk-show hostess whose signature line of fashion clothing was revealed to have been manufactured by waifs in squalid overseas sweatshops; the same Kathie Lee whose husband, football legend Frank Gifford, briefly took up with a flight attendant who arranged for a tabloid to publish grainy photographs of the tryst.

Here on the megascreen, though, Kathie Lee appears domestically serene. She's singing a tender-type love song titled "Forever and Ever," which (according to the graphic on the video) is available on a Disney record label and featured in a Disney full-length animated film. Glancing around the store, I notice I'm not the only customer frozen in place. The others display no snickering or outright derision, but rather a woozy glassiness of expression that dissolves only when Kathie Lee finishes her tune. Instantly she is replaced on the jumbo tube by Marilyn Manson, a flamboyant metalhead whose plangent ode to masochism puts an inexplicable bounce in my step. According to rock lore, several of Mr. Manson's ribs were surgically removed so he would be limber enough to perform oral sex upon himself. A future duet with Kathie Lee would seem out of the question, but one can always hope.

A few blocks away, Peep Land hangs on by cum-crusted fingernails. Inside . . . well, just try to get past the video racks. Sample: volumes one through five of *Ready to Drop*, an anthology featuring explicit (and occasionally team-style) sex with women in their third trimester of pregnancy. And that's not the worst of it, not even close. The shop's library of bodily-function videos is extensive, multilingual, and prominently displayed at eye level. Skin a-crawl, I am quickly out the door.

Revulsion is good. Revulsion is healthy. Each of us has limits, unarticulated boundaries of taste and tolerance, and sometimes we forget where they are. Peep Land is here to remind us; a fixed compass point by which we can govern our private behavior. Because being grossed out is essential to the human experience; without a perceived depravity, we'd have nothing against which to gauge the advance or decline of culture—our art, our music, our cinema, our books. Without sleaze, the yardstick shrinks at both ends. Team Rodent doesn't believe in sleaze, however, nor in old-fashioned revulsion. Square in the middle is where it wants us all to be, dependable consumers with predictable attitudes. The message, never stated but avuncularly implied, is that America's values ought to reflect those of the Walt Disney Company and not the other way around.

So there's a creepy comfort to be found amidst the donkey films and giant rubber dicks, a subversive triumph at unearthing such slag so near to Disney's golden portals. (Hey, Mickey, whistle on *this!*) Peep Land is important precisely because it's so irredeemable and because it cannot be transformed into anything but what it is. Slapping Disney's name on a joint like this would not elevate or enrich it even microscopically, or cause it to be taken for a shrine. Standing in Disney's path, Peep Land remains a gummy little cell of resistance.

And resistance is called for.

Insane Clown
Michael

IN 1996 THE WALT DISNEY COMPANY reported $18.7 billion in revenues, a thunderous 54 percent jump from the previous fiscal year. Its operating income was $3.3 billion (up 35 percent) and its net income was $1.5 billion (up 11 percent). In 1997 its revenues surpassed $20 billion.

Disney touches virtually every human being in America for a profit. That is rapidly becoming true as well in France, Spain, Germany, Japan, Great Britain, Australia, China, Mexico, Brazil, and Canada. Disney will devour the world the same way it devoured this country, starting first with the youth. Disney theme parks have drawn more than one billion visitors, mostly kids. Snag the children and everybody else follows—parents, politicians, even the press. *Especially* the press. We're all suckers for a good cartoon.

The money comes in a torrent, from Walt Disney Pictures, Touchstone, Caravan, Miramax, and Hollywood Pictures; from ABC, ESPN, the Disney Channel, Arts and Entertainment, the History Channel, and Lifetime; from Siskel and Ebert, Regis and Kathie Lee, and Monday Night Football; from nine TV stations, eleven AM radio stations, and ten FM radio stations; from home videos, stage plays, music publishing, book publishing, and seven daily newspapers; from the theme parks in Orlando, Anaheim, Tokyo, and Paris; from computer software, toys, and merchandise; from baseball and hockey franchises; from hotels, real-estate holdings, retail stores, shopping centers, housing developments, and soon even a cruise line.

At the core of Disney's platinum mine is entertainment. No other corporation has the capacity to crank out enough product to gorge the public maw. But as deep and bland as the mainstream has become, there are billions of dollars to be made outside of it; not everyone on the planet wants G-rated fare. When Disney targets adult tastes, it's careful to leave Walt's name off the credits. The same folks who brought you *101 Dal-matians*, a movie featuring adorable puppies, also brought you *Pulp Fiction*, a movie featuring junkies, hit men, and bondage freaks. The same folks who produce *Home Improvement*, a program about a wisecracking TV handyman, are also responsible for *Ellen*, a program about a wise-cracking lesbian.

"Mickey is a clean mouse," Walt Disney liked to say, but these days not everyone thinks so. Fif-teen million Southern Baptists, displeased with the content of certain Disney films and television programs—especially *Ellen*—profess to be boy-cotting. Protesters of like mind recently gathered at the entrance of Disney World to demonstrate against the company's policies of providing health insurance to partners of gay employees and holding an annual Gay Day at its Orlando theme parks. The demonstrators, who foisted pamphlets on carloads of incoming tourists, belonged to Operation Rescue National, an antiabortion group that is branching out to combat homosexuality. One marcher carried a sign that read "If You Love Jesus, Turn Around." Of course the tourists kept coming. Nothing short of flamethrowers would have stopped them. If anything is more irresistible than Jesus, it's Mickey.

That Disney is defying the morality police is a positive sign, one that somewhat softens my visceral antipathy toward Team Rodent. Given a choice between intolerant moralizers and unflinchingly ruthless profiteers, I'll have to stand with the Mouse every time. Many publicly held corporations would have caved at the first throaty outcry from fundamentalists, but Disney continues to stand firm. Obviously the Gay Day promotion makes enough dough and generates enough goodwill that Team Rodent can afford to ignore the Bible-thumpers.

The secret weapon is trust. Disney is the most trusted brand name in the history of marketing. It hooks us when we're little and never lets go, this unshakable faith that Disney is the best at knowing what's best. Who better to trust with Quentin Tarantino or a lesbian sitcom?

Remember also that the the company's granite base of consumers is a prosperous and relatively open-minded Middle America; a Middle America that still finds patience (and even loyalty) for Bill Clinton, a president reported to claim biblical license for soliciting extramarital blow jobs. Team Rodent knows the tolerance level of its audience because it *raised* its audience. The fundamentalists' "boycott" of Disney is doomed to flop because

Middle America isn't participating and doesn't, if you'll pardon the expression, give a rat's ass. Middle America completely trusts Mickey with sex, violence, and occasional unwholesomeness, as long as it's mildly entertaining.

Even so, one must wonder what the Disney brain trust was thinking in the summer of 1997 when, one week after the Southern Baptists denounced the company, its Hollywood Records division released an album called *The Great Milenko*. A brief but representative sample of lyrics:

> *I'd order you a drink then stir it with my*
> *   dick.*
> *And then to get your attention in a crowded*
> *   place*
> *I'd simply walk up and stick my nuts in your*
> *   face.*

Decidedly more Peep Land than Pat Boone. Other cuts on the album celebrated dismemberment, mutilation, forcible sodomy, necrophilia, and, in one instance, nonconsenting sex with a llama.

The group alleged to have written and performed these songs is named the Insane Clown Posse. The stars are presented as two white

"Detroit street rappers" calling themselves Violent J and Shaggy 2 Dope. On the album they are pictured as tongue-wagging jesters with painted faces. On the Internet they are pitched as "a celestial circus of lunacy, madness, and excess that travels through time and space to distort pleasant youthful memories into a horrific living night . . . these clowns carry axes instead of balloons."

Tupac Wayne Gacy!

The outcry over *The Great Milenko* was immediate and predictable. Six hours after the CD landed in music stores, Disney yanked it off the shelves. The company said that although the lyrics had been screened (and some songs cut) by its legal department, nobody had shared the material with the company's image-obsessed chairman, Michael D. Eisner.

At first it sounded plausible—*Milenko* bore all the signs of a bureaucractic fuckup, and wasn't Disney overdue? As Team Rodent's realm grows larger and more far-flung, airtight control becomes increasingly difficult to maintain. With so many creative and ambitious people on the payroll, it's inevitable that some will slip Eisner's reins.

But is that what really happened?

The *Milenko* CD was released and recalled on June 24, 1997. Other than a brief spate of news stories—"How'd Disney Ringmasters Let It Happen?" asked the *Los Angeles Times*—the incident faded quickly from the headlines. Disney appears not to have suffered at all, financially or imagewise. In fact, a case could be made that the company *benefited* from the publicity by responding so decisively. Never before had a hundred thousand units of anything been removed so swiftly from the reach of innocent consumers. It was as if Disney, under siege from the religious right, meant to reassure Middle America that it knew exactly where the lines of decency were drawn.

Which raises the intriguing possibility that *The Great Milenko* wasn't a blunder at all, but actually a sly public-relations trick. Suppose Disney was looking for a bone to throw to the fulminating Baptists. What better sacrifice than a tediously offensive rap album that nobody was going to buy anyway?

In retrospect, the likelihood of something so raunchy slipping past Eisner seems remote; the guy is legendary for micromanaging. Somebody high in the organization had to know *Milenko* was in the pipeline, because Disney was prepared for the ensuing uproar. Too prepared.

My theory: Eisner *is* the Insane Clown Posse.

Hell, those fabled "Imagineers" of his could have knocked off the liner notes on their lunch break, and had a hoot doing it. Who ever heard of white Detroit street rappers? And what's with the candy-ass *faux*-Kiss mascara? The songwriting is so strenuously witless that it's got to be a parody. How else to explain this ballad:

> *I got shot, the murder was heinous*
> *It went in my eyeball and out my anus.*

On the day Disney yanked the Posse's CD, Messrs. Violent J and Shaggy 2 Dope lashed out in cyberspace: "It all starts with a friendly big fluffy mouse named Mickey, who is really a lying rabid infested filthy rat in disguise."

I wouldn't be surprised if that turned out to be an Eisner riff, tweaking all of us who harbor such acid sentiments. Undoubtedly he's aware that his empire is the subject of percolating distrust, hatred, and even fear. The question he probably asks himself is why. What has Disney really done but brought joy, wonder, and laughter to billions of people? What accounts for the rising backlash?

Insane Clown Michael surely has his theories. My own virulence is rooted in this belief, based on what I've seen with my own eyes: Disney is so good at being good that it manifests an evil; so uniformly efficient and courteous, so dependably clean and conscientious, so unfailingly *entertaining* that it's unreal, and therefore is an agent of pure wickedness. Imagine promoting a universe in which raw Nature doesn't fit because it doesn't measure up; isn't safe enough, accessible enough, predictable enough, even beautiful enough for company standards. Disney isn't in the business of exploiting Nature so much as striving to improve upon it, constantly fine-tuning God's work.

Lakes, for instance. Florida's heartland is dappled with lovely tree-lined lakes, but the waters are often tea-colored from cypress bark. For post-card purposes, tea-colored water was deemed unsuitable for Disney World's centerpiece, Bay Lake, so in the early 1970s Team Rodent sprang into action—yanking out many of the cypresses, draining the lake, scraping out the bottom muck, replacing it with imported sand, then refilling the crater. All this was done to make the water bluish and therefore more inviting to tourists. For good measure, Disney even added beaches.

(My own Bay Lake fantasy: sneak in one night and dump a truckload of hungry bull gators in that lovely deep-blue water. I know friends who'd be thrilled to help, and who also have experience in the transport of large crocodilians. My conscience is all that's stopping me—the Magic Kingdom is not a safe place for a reptile, and I fear the alligators would be systematically hunted down and trapped, or worse.)

In recent years Team Rodent has become even less bashful and more technologically advanced at superimposing its own recreation-based reality. Disney-brand fun needs a script, and a script needs performing, and a performance needs a stage. No one is fussier about the production details than Team Rodent, and it pays off. Operating profit from Disney's theme parks and resorts has risen steeply in recent years and now accounts for more than 25 percent of company earnings.

One place the formula didn't work so well was France, where Disneyland Paris (then called Euro-Disney) opened at a cost of $4.4 billion in the spring of 1992. Dreary weather and a weak economy weren't the only reasons for disappointing attendance. The wine-loving French resented Disney's no-alcohol policy, while employees balked at the company's famous Aryan-android dress code, which forbids makeup, nail polish, and facial hair. Critics and commentators despaired that Disneyland Paris was a blight on native French culture, and the leftist newspaper *Libération* harshly dubbed it "Mouse-witz." At one point the park was losing the equivalent of $1 million a day, and was reported to be on the verge of closing. It was saved by a complicated financial restructuring and a grudging decision by Disney executives to act more European and loosen up the rules. Today wine is served at Disneyland Paris restaurants, and revenues at the park are rising.

Beyond the rare movie flop, Disney is unaccustomed to failure. It prizes its reputation for profitability almost as much as its reputation for wholesome entertainment. No other company so zealously endeavors to live up to its own hype—and manages to come so close. Success after success has turned Team Rodent into a ravenous, fearless beast, and that's why many of us now cheer those infrequent occasions when it is rebuffed, humbled, or gored.

Bull Run

DATELINE: HAYMARKET, VIRGINIA, November 1993.

For many months the Walt Disney Company has been anonymously snapping up property in the Piedmont, just as it did many years ago outside Orlando. This time, though, Disney's got something different in mind: a 150-acre amusement park with a history theme, to attract day-tripping tourists from Washington, D.C. Also in the works are a campground, a golf course and resort, twenty-five hundred new residential homes, and a boggling two million square feet of office and commercial space. The three-thousand-acre, $650 million development is announced with fanfare and the promise of many new jobs—and within months comes under blistering attack from all over the country.

The outcome proved genuinely historic, though not in the way CEO Eisner foresaw. At issue was the proposed theme park's proximity to the Manassas National Battlefield, scene of the battles of Bull Run. Although the nucleus of Disney's "America Project" was to be six miles from the Civil War memorial, many Virginians felt it was close enough to be a desecration. This time it wasn't Nature but American history that Disney sought to polish up and market as a fun ride. Opponents said Manassas was no place for a massive theme park/golf resort/subdivision, and predicted the surrounding hillsides would be ruined by the same type of tacky runaway sprawl that had surrounded Walt Disney World. The rape of Orlando was invoked constantly as a battle cry.

Another sore point was money, specifically taxpayers' money. Disney attorneys had nonchalantly demanded more than $200 million in state funds for new roads and highway improvements around the park and office complex. Meanwhile the residents of Prince William County would be expected to contribute another $75 million for water, sewage, landscaping, and other necessities. "It was not a request, it was not respectful and it was confidently stated," recalled Prince William County executive Jim Mullen, writing in *Public Management* magazine.

He and other planners visited their Florida counterparts to quiz them about how Team Rodent operates. "Arrogant, demanding, aloof, confident, efficient, powerful, successful and profitable were the words used to describe Disney," Mullen reported. But in Orange County, as in Prince William, the prevailing view was that government was wise to make Disney comfortable, even if groveling was required; anything less could jeopardize an economic windfall for the community. So Mullen and his colleagues began working nonstop to improve Disney's master plan in ways that all sides might find acceptable. The task would prove impossible in the face of a growing outcry from environmentalists, Civil War historians, and nearby landowners, some of whom had influential political connections.

Despite the resistance, in March 1994 the Virginia General Assembly approved $163.2 million in benefits for Disney. Almost immediately a citizens' group filed two lawsuits in an effort to halt the America Project. Eisner assured the *Washington Post* that the Walt Disney Company was solidly committed to its northern Virginia theme park:

"If the people think we will back off, they are mistaken."

They weren't mistaken. Three months after Eisner's vow, Disney backed off. The company was taking a publicity beating worldwide and could not overcome the perception that Mickey and Minnie soon would be dancing on the graves of Civil War heroes. So, only days after $130 million in road-building funds had been authorized for the America Project, Disney decided to retreat from Prince William County.

Today Virginians still argue about whether the megadevelopment would have been a blessing or a debacle. It's undeniably true that some folks would have gotten rich, because that's what happens when Mickey comes to town. It's also true that lots of folks soon would have found their town unrecognizable: congested, noisy, tackified, and tourist-trammeled. As for the Manassas battlefield memorial, the six-mile distance would have provided no buffer whatsoever from the Disney outfall. *One hundred miles* is too close, if the desired atmosphere is a dignified quiet.

Good for all those people who fought back against Team Rodent. It was about time somebody did.

Enough Orlandos, already.

Republic of
Walt

IN THE MID-1960S farmers, ranchers, and other rural land holders in central Florida began receiving inquiries from prospective buyers. The offers were fair, though not high enough to attract suspicion. Even at $200 an acre, most owners were happy to sell. The transactions seemed routine, and it was a while before folks realized what was happening.

By then, roughly twenty-four thousand acres had been acquired in methodical quilt-patch purchases by Walt Disney Productions. Realizing that the price of land would have shot up if his involvement were known, Walt Disney had kept his role a strictly guarded secret. The payoff was an incredible real-estate coup that eventually would transform forty-three square miles of pastures, woods, and swamps into the world's most popular tourist destination.

Walt died five years before Disney World opened, but its future was secure. That's because Florida's legislators blitheringly agreed to give the company virtually whatever it wanted, and the main thing it wanted was autonomy: a private government for constructing and managing an amusement park. Thus was born the Reedy Creek Improvement District, an innocuous-sounding title that belies unheard-of powers. "The Vatican with mouse ears," says Richard Foglesong, a Rollins College professor and longtime Disney watcher.

Reedy Creek takes in all the land purchased by Walt's secret agents in the 1960s. The district is "governed" by a supervisory board elected by the landowners, meaning the Walt Disney Company. Its borders contain two shell municipalities, Lake Buena Vista and Bay Lake, which have a combined permanent population of fewer than fifty souls, mostly company executives and their families. Everybody in Orlando knows that Reedy Creek is Disney and Disney is Reedy Creek, although for legal reasons both claim to be separate. That's because Florida requires municipal governments to conduct their business in public, and for competitive reasons Team Rodent would rather not.

Never before or since has such outlandish dominion been given to a private corporation. Disney runs its own utilities. It administers its own planning and zoning. It composes its own building codes and employs its own inspectors. It maintains its own fire department. It even has the authority to levy taxes.

Florida's starstruck lawmakers didn't stop there. They also gave Disney's puppet government the authority to build its own international airport and even a nuclear power plant—neither of which the company has needed . . . yet. Reedy Creek is further empowered to have cemeteries, schools, a police department, and a criminal justice system—services that Disney has so far chosen not to assume.

Reedy Creek does, however, "contract" with Disney for an eight-hundred-member security force that patrols Epcot, the Magic Kingdom, hotels, shops, restaurants, and roads—everywhere on company property. The "hosts" and "hostesses" wear blue uniforms and carry badges, just like real cops. Legally they're not, although they sometimes forget.

Two friends of mine, Charlie and Cheryl

Freeman, once took their son and daughter to Church Night at Disney World. They went on a bus with seventeen other children and several parents. Charlie drove.

Outside Tomorrowland, the Freemans had a run-in with another group of youngsters on an escalator. The kids were swearing loudly. When Charlie asked them to stop, one of them swung a leg and caught Cheryl in the ribs. Charlie thought it was an accident until the kid got in his face and said, "What's your problem, you fucking geek!"

That's when Charlie "grabbed him by the breastbone and pushed him back." Moments later Charlie found himself in the custody of Disney security guards. The kid said Charlie had tried to choke him. Charlie denied it. "I was wrong to touch him," he said, "but he kicked my wife." And there were witnesses.

It didn't matter. The guards took Charlie to a small room, where he was interviewed and photographed with a Polaroid camera. Then he was escorted out the front gate and informed he was banned from Disney World for twelve months. His picture would be posted, the guards warned, and he would be arrested for trespassing if he was spotted anywhere at the park.

On the long drive back to Jacksonville, Charlie

kept saying, "I got thrown out of Disney World on *Church Night!*" He was so angry that he phoned the newspaper when he got home. Columnist Robert Blade wrote about the incident in the *Florida Times-Union*. Readers clipped the article and mailed protests to Disney. Soon afterward Charlie received a letter from the company's chief of security: "This is to notify you that, effective immediately, the trespass warning against you for Walt Disney World Resort Complex has been lifted."

Officially Disney says its security forces work closely with local police. A sheriff's deputy is assigned to the grounds to make arrests or otherwise assist the guards, if needed. All crimes in the Reedy Creek Improvement District are supposed to be reported promptly to law enforcement authorities. That doesn't always happen, due to Disney's fanatical obsession with secrecy.

In 1991 the company learned that one of its wardrobe assistants was spying on female performers at Cinderella's Castle. The young man would masturbate while surreptitiously videotaping the women as they changed costumes.

One phone call to the local sheriff's office could have ended the peep show, but Disney security officers chose to conduct their own surveillance, which went on for three months. According to court records, the company deliberately didn't inform the women at the castle about the investigation, and in fact permitted the secret taping to continue. Eventually Disney's security guards photographed the wanker in the act, confronted him, and got a confession. He later was arrested by a sheriff's deputy, who'd allegedly overheard employees talking about the illegal videos in the coffee room of the Disney security office.

Six female dancers from the Kids of the Kingdom chorus later sued, demanding $37.5 million in damages. They asserted that the dressing areas in Cinderella's Castle had been plagued by Peeping Toms who carved small eyeholes in the walls, and that Disney had known about the problem.

As for the sting operation, in which the company used its own video camera, the dancers charged that on January 8, 1992, Disney security allowed the suspect "to remain in this hidden place, masturbating, observing and videotaping the female Kids of the Kingdom cast in states of partial or total nudity for over one hour and 15 minutes and did not apprehend [him] until the female performers left for their 11 o'clock performance."

Disney acknowledged it didn't tell the performers they were being spied upon, but the company said it acted properly. Moreover, the company preposterously claimed the dancers had no cause to sue, because they had "a diminished expectation of privacy in their particular job requirements and . . . therefore knowingly assumed the risk of the matters alleged."

In refusing to dismiss the lawsuit, the judge said ordinary citizens would find the company's conduct "outrageous." On the eve of trial, Disney's attorneys settled the case with the Kids of the Kingdom for an undisclosed sum.

Litigation and rotten publicity often go hand in hand, and Team Rodent is ever-wary of both. Several employees caught exposing themselves to tourists have been quietly fired but not turned over to the police. Yet even in such a rigidly monitored setting, events sometimes occur that can't be covered up.

On the night of August 31, 1994, Disney World guards spotted two young men goofing around on the roof of a covered walkway at the Contemporary Resort. The young men quickly scrambled to the ground, ran to a pickup truck, and sped away. A Disney security van pursued, its red lights flashing.

The chase reached speeds approaching eighty miles per hour. A mile outside Disney World's gates, the pickup crashed, killing the passenger, eighteen-year-old Robb Sipkema.

In Florida, all traffic deaths are investigated by the state highway patrol. The troopers assigned to the Sipkema case found Disney not at all helpful. Incredibly, the company refused to let them interview Susan Buckland, the "security hostess" who was at the wheel of the van during the pursuit. Disney also declined to release transcripts of the radio communications between Buckland and the company dispatcher during the fatal chase. The lead investigator, Florida Highway Patrol Trooper Scott Walter, complained to the *Orlando Sentinel* that Disney officials "would only release the information that wouldn't hurt them."

Robb Sipkema's parents sued, setting off a legal battle that has partially raised the curtain on Disney's private government. The Sipkemas charged that the security guard caused their son's death by pursuing the pickup truck, even though she was not a sworn law enforcement officer. Buckland said she did nothing wrong and never drove her vehicle off Disney property that night.

Florida has a broad public-records law that applies to all state and local government entities—

including, one would reasonably assume, the Reedy Creek Improvement District. Because Disney provides policelike services for Reedy Creek, the family of Robb Sipkema demanded a copy of the company's security manual and policy on traffic control.

Disney said no. Its attorneys asserted that, as a private corporation, Disney wasn't required to open its records.

Eventually Team Rodent voluntarily produced the security manual, but the Sipkemas pressed for more files. Their lawyers noted that Disney and Reedy Creek were one and the same, and that Disney security guards acted as a de facto police force. The "hosts" and "hostesses" conducted traffic stops, answered 911 calls, and investigated crimes "to the point of arrest." When communicating over the radio, they even spoke in the same 10-codes as real cops.

It wasn't enough to convince Orange County Circuit Judge Belvin Perry Jr. He sided with Disney, ruling that its law enforcement activities at Reedy Creek were part of a private security arrangement—in other words, a contract with itself. Bottom line: The public, including the Sipkemas, would not be allowed to see internal company documents.

The decision rankled lots of folks familiar with the Reedy Creek charade, especially those in Orange County. In 1990 they had competed with the district for $57.7 million in tax-free bonds. Orange officials needed to raise money for low-income housing. Reedy Creek wanted to expand the sewage-treatment capacity for Disney's fast-growing theme parks.

The county's poor lost out. Mickey and Minnie won.

So if Disney enjoys the powers of municipal government, including the right to sell tax-free bonds, shouldn't it be governed by the same laws of open disclosure? In 1997 an appeals court said no, upholding the ruling against Robb Sipkema's family, the state attorney general, and several newspapers that had joined the lawsuit. The panel of judges agreed with the trial court's puzzling position that Disney guards aren't like real police and perform only basic "night watchman" duties.

Which apparently have been broadened to include high-speed car chases of suspected trespassers. "Outrageous," said John Hargrove, one of the lawyers who argued for the side of the Sipkemas. "Talk about a family getting screwed."

Without access to Disney's files, the Sipkemas

hit a wall. They have dropped the lawsuit over their son's death.

Meanwhile, the *Orlando Sentinel* reports that the flashing lights on Disney's security vehicles have been changed from red to amber, so as not to be taken for those of real cop cars. In addition, Disney's uniformed guards—the "hosts" and "hostesses"—no longer use *Dragnet*-style police codes when talking over the radio.

Goofy's gendarmes still do an impressive job of keeping order, though. Every now and then reality intrudes—a shoplifter, a flasher, a fistfight between tourists, an accidental fall, a fatal heart attack on the Space Mountain roller coaster. Such incidents are handled with astounding swiftness and discretion, the scene usually cleared and back to normal within minutes. Team Rodent's crisis squads appear ready for every imaginable emergency.

Well, maybe not *every* emergency. As I write this, a potentially breathtaking drama is unfolding within stalking distance of Adventureland. A full-grown African lioness has escaped from a roadside zoo called JungleLand, on State Road 192. Also known as the Irlo Bronson Memorial Highway, it's one of Florida's all-time unsightliest thoroughfares, crammed with T-shirt shops, fast-food joints, cut-rate car rental lots, bargain motels, and souvenir kiosks. The road looks like this for one reason: It's on the way to Disney World.

The escaped cat is called Nala, named (predictably) after a lioness character in Disney's animated blockbuster *The Lion King*. The real-life Nala has vanished into a stretch of heavy woods off 192, not far from an International House of Pancakes. Teams of armed searchers and wildlife officers are trying to track the animal, while journalists from all over the world cluster in safety along the shoulder of the highway. Even the major TV networks are keeping tabs on the slapdash safari. Like other Florida newspapers, the *Miami Herald* has published a locator map showing the estimated proximity of the fugitive lioness to the Magic Kingdom, Epcot, and the Disney-MGM Studios. Presumably this information will help tourists weigh the risk of a visit and plan their routes accordingly. Indeed, much of the news coverage deals with speculation that the big cat is making her way toward Disney property.

Sweet Jesus, just imagine: the hot-blooded 450-pound namesake of a Disney cartoon lion, bounding down Main Street U.S.A. (perhaps during the nightly SpectroMagic Parade!) and with one lightning swipe of a paw taking down

Goofy or Pluto, or maybe one of those frigging chipmunks. A harrowing primal eruption—and Disney could blame no one but itself!

Because Nala wouldn't be loose in Orlando if there was no JungleLand, and there would be no JungleLand if there was no Walt Disney World.

So the escaped lioness has a secret fan club that believes a split second of raw predation might be good for Team Rodent's soul. And while it is being widely reported that the big cat is declawed, I choose not to believe it.

Forgive us our fantasies.

The Puppy King

IN DECEMBER 1997 DISNEY chairman Michael D. Eisner exercised company stock options that brought him $565 million in a single swoop. The notion of attaching such a sum to one man's job is both obscene and hilarious on its face, yet it's pointless to debate whether or not Eisner deserves it. He got the dough.

It happened in the same month that *Business Week* chose Disney's board of directors as the worst in America. The reason: Many seemed to have been handpicked not so much for their business expertise as for their loyalty to the autocratic Eisner. Among the company's directors are his personal architect, his personal attorney, the principal of his children's elementary school, and seven current and former Disney executives. "Fantastic" is how Eisner has described his choices for the board, but critics say it's a meek and malleable group. That's precisely what was needed to sit still for the ludicrous $75 million platinum parachute given to Michael Ovitz as compensation for fourteen whole months as president of the Walt Disney Company. Hiring the Hollywood superagent had been Eisner's idea, but the decision to part was said to be mutual. Eisner is so hyperactively involved with Team Rodent's many enterprises that Ovitz had been left with not enough to do.

As exorbitant as the mistake turned out to be, Disney could easily afford it. The company has experienced astounding growth in the fourteen years since Insane Clown Michael's arrival, and he's not shy about rattling off all the new ventures: radio and TV stations, cable systems, newspapers, books, home video, theatrical productions, computer games and programs, professional sports teams, and of course Times Square. Of all the new endeavors, the most expensive and ambitious was the acquisition of Capital Cities/ABC and its affiliated broadcast networks, which instantly gave Disney a huge self-marketing apparatus.

Perhaps Eisner is a true genius—a visionary, a brilliant motivator, a magnetic communicator. If so, you wouldn't know it from the following communiqué, which Eisner sent to Disney shareholders and employees as part of the 1996 annual report:

> Last week I was trying to write this letter in the living room of my family's farmhouse in Saxtons River, Vermont, where I have been going for the Thanksgiving holidays for 35 years. At my side was the cover of the annual report with its hundred and one dalmatians staring at me, begging me to begin. But I was stuck. The Florida/Florida State football game, broadcast on ABC, was in the background and I found myself looking up every time I saw a McDonald's/dalmatian commercial. Cute dalmatians everywhere, each one saying, "Get to work." But then there was this overwhelmingly positive review from a Boston television station for our movie *The English Patient* that I had to listen to, and of course I had to take a call from Florida reporting excellent attendance at Walt Disney World. I then called our

European headquarters to learn that *The Hunchback of Notre Dame* opened with extraordinary results in 12 territories, including France, Germany, Belgium, Switzerland and Holland. This motivated me to make more calls: dialing, still not typing. I found out *The Rock* would likely become the biggest home video rental of all time and that *Toy Story*'s video release was selling at superb rates. Finally I got the call that unlocked my procrastination. *101 Dalmatians* was a smash. It would break every possible record at the box office for the Thanksgiving break. It was huge, massive! Now, as soon as the Mighty Ducks hockey game against the Chicago Blackhawks at the Pond in Anaheim on ESPN was over, I would finally begin to work. We wouldn't have to change the cover of our annual report! The *Dalmatians* had come through!

Obviously, Eisner wrote the letter himself—no PR flack in his right mind would've sent out such hyperbolic twaddle. But as fulsome and windy as it is, the letter fairly depicts the company's fast-tightening grip on the global entertainment culture. One cannot overstate Disney's reach, and there's no better example than Eisner's superhyped *101 Dalmatians*.

As soon as word got out that Disney was producing a live-action remake of its popular 1961 feature-length cartoon, puppy mills across America began breeding dalmatians like rats. It was a sure bet. Once the movie opened, thousands upon thousands of parents went shopping for puppies to put under the Christmas tree for their smitten children. Just as Eisner had bubbled: cute dalmatians everywhere!

Unfortunately, dalmatians aren't the ideal breed for every family. They can be high-strung, snappish, and intolerant of youngsters. In other words: Not cute. Less than a year after the film's release, animal shelters and Humane Societies got swamped with young dogs that had failed to deliver the cuddliness promised by their lovable big-screen counterparts. South Florida shelters reported a 35 percent increase in the number of dalmatians, many of them facing a sad and predictable fate. The story was the same all across the country.

Don't get me wrong. I'm not laying a single euthanized puppy at the feet of Michael Eisner. The parents who dashed out to buy those dogs should have known better; they should have steeled themselves against sentiment. They should have known that captivation is the mission of a Disney film, a Disney theme park, a Disney merchandise store, a Disney *anything*. Charm, captivate, and conquer—that's how the empire advances. In the case of *101 Dalmatians*, Mom and Dad's imagination got as carried away as the kids'.

It's easy to sympathize. When I was sixteen Disney released a movie called *Rascal*, the adventures of a mischievous yet adorable baby raccoon. My own parents sensibly forbade me from sneaking into the woods and capturing my own ring-tailed varmint, but shortly after college I acquired one. Picture the scene in a small two-bedroom apartment: father, mother, one three-year-old toddler, and one wild raccoon. An absolutely adorable critter, as advertised, until the day it rebelled against the mildest of discipline, climbed up on my portable Smith-Corona, and (in a gesture that transcended mischief) took a long hard piss.

The pathetic truth is that, like millions of others, I'd succumbed to the spell of Disney make-believe. Real raccoons don't behave like movie raccoons, any more than real dogs behave like movie dogs.

As cynically as one might appraise Eisner's cornball letter to Disney stockholders, no evidence suggests he was unmoved by later news reports about all the homeless and neglected puppies generated by *101 Dalmatians*. Even before the film opened, the company publicly had tried to warn people against impulsively rushing out to a pet shop.

It was money that would have been more wisely spent on a fluffy toy dalmatian at a Disney Store, not that Insane Clown Michael was thinking along such mercenary lines. In fairness, he didn't invent Disney's overpowering brand of make-believe. He simply took it worldwide.

Fantasy
Fantasy Island

IN A FEW MONTHS, an eighty-five-thousand-ton ocean liner will be launched from a shipyard in Marghera, Italy. The ship is decorated like no other of its kind. Etched into the steep prow is a portrait of that renowned mariner, Mickey Mouse. At the other end: a fifteen-foot likeness of Goofy, swinging from a boatswain's chair while pretending to paint the stern. The ship's horn is specially tuned to play "When You Wish upon a Star."

The name of this extraordinary vessel is *Disney Magic*, Team Rodent's maiden venture into the lucrative cruise-line trade. Carrying twenty-four hundred passengers (most of whom have spent the preceding days at Disney World), the ship will serve as both a floating extension of the Orlando theme park and a marketing barge. Nightclubs, theaters, swimming pools, and spas will offer no refuge from Magic Kingdom characters; in one restaurant, "live" walls will display Disney art evolving from sketch to full animation.

Even the lifeboats will be tricked out—painted bright yellow and styled to match the old vessels depicted in *Steamboat Willie*. Undoubtedly the workmanship will be top-notch and authentic-looking, but imagine yourself far out at sea aboard a sinking ocean liner. Would your first choice of a rescue vessel be a lifeboat whose design was inspired by a 1928 cartoon?

The *Disney Magic* will leave Port Canaveral for three- or four-day excursions to Nassau and Castaway Cay, billed as the company's "private Bahamian island." Here passengers will debark and frolic in a manicured tropical setting, with separate beaches provided for kids, families, and adults (Disney is hoping for a big newlywed trade).

While other cruise lines have purchased small Bahamian islands as quickie stopovers, not many can boast the lively history of Disney's—a history the company is unlikely to share with its seagoing passengers. "Castaway Cay" is the newly Imagineered name for the island, but locals know it as Gorda Cay. It was a very busy place in the 1970s and 1980s, the main draw being a secluded and unpatrolled airfield, upon which many tons of marijuana, Quaaludes, and cocaine were landed en route to the U.S. mainland.

During that era Gorda Cay fell under the control of an American smuggler named Frank Barber, who ferried the dope up from Colombia and used the island for storage and refueling. Later the stuff was flown to small landing strips in south Florida, a nocturnal enterprise that owed much of its success to Barber's recruitment and bribery of a U.S. drug enforcement agent named Jeffrey Scharlatt. Both men wound up in prison. Shortly after their operation was exposed, a Commission of Inquiry convened in Nassau to investigate drug smuggling and corruption throughout the commonwealth; Gorda Cay was listed as one of the favorite stopovers for international dope runners.

The island's notoriety presented no serious public-relations hurdle for Disney, which merely changed the name after buying the place. It's a small illustration of how Team Rodent untarnishes reality, acquiring and recasting to its own designs. Be certain that the company's security forces scoured Gorda Cay and left no coconut unturned, in case Mr. Barber and his colleagues had stashed some goodies prior to their departure.

Beachcombing tourists in Fort Lauderdale are excited to stumble across the occasional scuttled bale, but in a Disney biosphere there's no place for such surprises. I'll bet a new past is being ghost-written for "Castaway Cay"—a past richly populated with conquistadors or perhaps shipwrecked pirates, whom Disney copywriters would regard as more colorful and less menacing than modern smugglers of cocaine and bootleg methaqualone.

Escape is what most ordinary folks want and deserve—escape from the threat of dope, guns, crime, poverty, pollution, random violence, urban unrest. So why not a carefree Castaway Cay? What's the harm? Maybe none. Be assured that the flora and fauna of the former Gorda Cay never received such tender loving care as they do now under Disney.

Still, there's something offensive to the spirit about taking a perfectly interesting little island and giving it a movie-style makeover to amuse the visiting sightseers. Trim the trees, groom the beaches, add a fleet of Jet Skis and a row of "massage cabanas"—hey, mon, you be jammin'! Commercializing paradise is a tradition nearly as old as the tropics, but Disney has pushed it into an insidious new realm. At least in Nassau or Kingston or even Key West you can poke around and find back streets and alleys that aren't on the tour, real neighborhoods with real people instead of "cast members." But on a Disney island you get only Disney adventure; everything you see and do is part of the show. So on Castaway Cay there's no chance of coming across a native fisherman mending his nets and cussing up a storm. On the other hand, there's also no chance of getting nicked by a pickpocket or groped by a hooker.

That trade-off is acceptable to millions of vacationers who don't mind the fake, as long as it's fun and safe. And nobody provides a safer, more closely supervised brand of carefree than Team Rodent. Whether you're on a Disney ocean liner or a Disney log flume or the eighteenth fairway of a Disney golf course, you can be pretty sure nobody's going to sneak up and stick a real .45 in your back. That's not just a perception, it's a fact—and one reason that Disney's image as a benign enchanter-protector is now embedded in the collective parental psyche. It also helps explain why anyone would sign up for a *lottery* to purchase a house in a Disney-designed subdivision: They probably remember how happy and secure they feel inside the Magic Kingdom.

Future World

ONE OF WALT DISNEY'S unfulfilled dreams was a model city of the future, which he called Epcot (Experimental Prototype Community of Tomorrow). It would be home to twenty thousand residents and offer never-before-seen technology for ultramodern family living. After Walt's death, the company scrapped the original idea for Epcot. Only the name was saved, given to a futuristic-looking wing of the Orlando theme park, where the attractions are sponsored by General Motors, AT&T, and other major U.S. corporations.

A few years ago Disney dusted off the concept of a functioning tomorrowland and called it Celebration. (The name, it's not surprising to learn, was selected by Michael Eisner and his wife.) Walt might recognize the place, though not as his futuristic bubble of a community. With its neat, narrow streets and neotraditional architecture, Celebration invokes nothing so much as a small-town neighborhood of the 1950s, remembered overfondly. The houses, which feature wooden shutters and open porches, could have been lifted off the lot of TV's *Leave It to Beaver*. Celebration boasts a school, a town hall, a library, parks, even a "downtown" within walking distance of most of the homes. Yet by no means is it a self-contained cell. All serious shopping is done in distant malls, and most folks who live in Celebration make the grinding daily commute to jobs in Orlando. There are no monorails or bullet trains or electric cars—just ordinary gas-slurping sport-utility vehicles and sedans.

The most ultramodern thing about Celebration is the price: from $200,000 to more than $1 million for a house, and as much as $80,000 for an undeveloped quarter-acre lot. That's a load of money for what is basically just another snugly platted wedge of suburbia—except it was designed, built, and marketed by Disney. Consequently, families who'd never otherwise dream of moving into a Florida subdivision are snapping up homes in Celebration, paying from 25 to 40 percent more than their neighbors in comparable projects along State Road 192.

It's a striking testament to the allure of the Disney name, and also to the childlike trust it elicits in boomer-era consumers. About five thousand people competed in a lottery for the first 350 homes to be built at Celebration. The company is counting on such exuberant fealty to grow its microplanned development to a buildout population of twenty thousand. Located five miles from Disney World, the new housing subdivision has gotten such a buzz that it actually draws tourists, who may purchase a Celebration wristwatch for $63 or a keepsake pen for half as much. Amazingly, some do.

Prospective settlers aren't wrong to believe that because it's a Disney enterprise, Celebration will be different from other Sunbelt suburbs. It surely is. New residents receive a book of detailed rules governing many aspects of life, from the color of one's house to the pattern of one's shrubbery to acceptable parking practices. There's a homeowners association with an elected board, but all decisions are subject to veto by Disney (presumably in the event the town is someday infiltrated by political hotheads). Most residents don't seem to mind the fussy rules or the company's large role in their lives; after all, order, neatness, and safety are precisely what they were shopping for in a neighborhood. And most of them plainly trust Disney to do the right thing. It's a recurring theme in published interviews with new Celebrationites: They grew up with Disney. Disney stands for quality. When Disney does something, it does it right. Disney would never screw them over.

Of course, nothing in Disney lore points to a special expertise in residential home construction, yet fifteen hundred people have so far entrusted the roofs over their heads to a company best known for thrill rides and cartoon movies. It isn't the first time.

In the 1980s Disney involved itself in another planned community, with calamitous results. The place was called Country Walk, a subdivision of gabled upscale houses and condominiums in southern Dade County. The development was built by the Arvida Corp., which was owned by Disney until 1987, when it sold its holdings, including 322 homes, condos, and lots.

Five years later Hurricane Andrew smashed into south Florida, and Country Walk was blown to pieces. Hundreds of residents were left homeless and shell-shocked. Many of the wood-frame houses that disintegrated during the storm had been built during Disney's corporate stewardship. In the debris, experts found ample evidence of sloppy construction practices. The bracing on some houses was so inadequate that the gables had been literally sucked off the roofs by high winds. Engineers discovered rows and rows of nails that were purely decorative, having cleanly missed the trusses they were supposed to secure.

Homeowners began filing lawsuits against Disney and Arvida, and prosecutors opened a criminal investigation. Although Disney asserted it had done nothing wrong, it eventually settled a class-action lawsuit out of court. Since most of the homes had been fully insured against storm damage, the owners agreed to accept $7,500 each from Arvida and Disney—pocket change for the mammoth entertainment conglomerate, and a smart way to put an end to the nasty headlines.

But not everyone in Country Walk went along with the deal. Alex and Helen Major, whose four-bedroom home was ripped apart by the hurricane, wanted a jury to hear their case. They withdrew from the class-action suit and pressed ahead on their own.

In the fall of 1996, with the trial date

approaching, something strange happened. Disney's attorneys succeeded in convincing Dade County Circuit Judge Celeste Muir to leave the company's name out of the case—not the company, just the name. Jurors would never hear the word *Disney* mentioned in open court.

Alex Major was miffed. Before he'd decided to purchase his house, Country Walk salesmen had juiced up their pitch by invoking the magical Disney reputation. "They told me Disney was the owner of Arvida," Major recalled to the *Miami Herald*. "You trust people when they tell you how good they are. I've been going to Disney since I was a little kid."

When Major's attorney stood before the jury, he must have been tempted to wisecrack about the Mickey Mouse construction at Country Walk. He didn't. Instead he presented aerial photos documenting how Arvida had hurried the project to meet heavy sales demand. The Majors' house, for example, had been completed three months *before* the required building permits were issued.

One of the strongest witnesses was Bob Sheets, a respected meteorologist and former chief of the National Hurricane Center. He testified that Country Walk suffered significantly more damage than nearby subdivisions, under identical storm conditions. There could be only one explanation: Lousy workmanship.

Disney and Arvida insisted its houses were built to code and properly inspected. Company lawyers said the Majors should have been aware of the hurricane risk in south Florida and should have done a better job boarding up in advance of the high winds.

Jurors didn't agree. They ordered Arvida and two subcontractors to pay $106,675 to the Majors. Would the sum have been higher if the jury had been allowed to hear of Disney's involvement? Obviously that's what Team Rodent feared; the same famous name that helped sell all those Country Walk houses could, conversely, amplify a jury's sentiment that the buyers had been tricked or betrayed.

Solution: Completely erase the word *Disney* from the debate. After all, hadn't it been nearly ten years since the company had sold Arvida? It was an audacious argument, but the judge bought it. As for the criminal inquiry, Arvida/Disney was never charged. In fact, few builders were busted in the wake of Hurricane Andrew, despite ample evidence of reckless and incompetent construction. The state attorney's office said the statute of limitations ran out before its investigations were complete.

The folks in Celebration, Florida, don't have as much to fret about, storm-wise, as those who bought houses in Country Walk. Orlando sits many miles inland from either the Gulf of Mexico or the Atlantic Ocean, and it is unlikely to receive the brunt of a major summer hurricane.

But if Disney's subdivision-of-the-future was to be ravaged by some other natural disaster— say, tornadoes of the fierce kind that ripped through nearby Kissimmee in February 1998— rescue duties would not fall to the Reedy Creek Improvement District. That's because Disney has deannexed Celebration from its main property, a legal maneuver ensuring that sovereign Reedy Creek will remain largely unpopulated, and therefore safe from the uncertainties of democracy.

Whistle While
We Work

TEAM RODENT COULDN'T have hijacked the culture without first enlisting the press, which is easier than you think. In 1965 the publisher of the *Orlando Sentinel* learned that Walt Disney was secretly acquiring property for a giant amusement park. Walt vowed to scuttle the deal if word leaked out, so the newspaper obligingly sat on the story until the deal was done. The embargo guaranteed Disney the lowest land prices, and also a minimum of public inquiry about the possible impact of the project. Florida would never be the same.

Conversely, when Team Rodent *wants* publicity, it's easy to get. Every major Disney enterprise becomes news, and the company's spokespeople are adept at wooing journalists without insulting their integrity. The town of Celebration had home buyers waiting in line because the development got coast-to-coast press attention, most of it favorable. The same is true for Disney's new cruise line, its wild-animal theme park, and even the porn-purging Times Square incursion. Journalists aren't as resistant to smooth corporate charm as they'd like you to believe; free food and an open bar always help.

Better than any other company, Disney understands the true face of the American media: hollow-cheeked, restless, and disenchanted. Most news operations in this country are small, parochial, and tightfisted. The people employed there are woefully underpaid, overworked, and often bored out of their skulls—ripe candidates for a junket to beautiful sun-drenched Florida, especially in the wintertime.

Many major-market papers and broadcast stations forbid their reporters from taking freebies, and in a perfect world that would be the rule for all journalists. The reason is obvious. We're the first ones to crucify a politician for accepting undisclosed favors from cronies or special interests. For us to do the same would be hypocritical. The public could, and should, assume that a free vacation might influence a reporter's objectivity, just as it might influence a congressman's vote. It's damn hard to stay neutral about somebody when you're sipping their merlot and sucking down their jumbo shrimp. Incorruptible or not, reporters shouldn't put themselves in a situation that raises the question.

That's the theory, anyway. The reality is something else, as Team Rodent well knows. Deep down, the average journalist isn't so different from the average autoworker or the average postal carrier or the average Super Bowl MVP. Who wouldn't jump at the chance for a trip to Disney World?

The company is gung-ho on anniversaries, these being splendid occasions for inviting battalions of reporters to Orlando for weekends of high-end gluttony and mooching. Depending upon how cheap your newspaper or broadcast station happens to be, Disney is prepared to pay for just about everything, from air travel to lodging to entertainment. Company publicists say they're not trying to buy us off with free food and fun; rather, they're merely broadening Disney's exposure by reaching out to interested media outlets—a coy hedge, but still closer to an honest defense than you'll get from some reporters.

Those who take the free trips say they're too

ethical to be compromised by a plane ticket or a steak dinner or a toy dalmatian for the kids. These indignant assertions, made with a straight face, are hard to believe when you see the stampede of foam-flecked Fourth Estate freeloaders at a Disney dinner buffet.

I witnessed it myself in October 1986, which I believe was the last time I set foot in the Magic Kingdom. The dual occasion was the fifteenth anniversary of the opening of Walt Disney World and the bicentennial of the U.S. Constitution. Neither qualified as much of a news event, but that scarcely mattered; the ploy of marrying a blatantly commercial promotion to a patriotic anniversary is vintage Disney. Former chief justice Warren Burger was flown in to legitimize the celebration—the fact it was almost a year shy of the actual bicentennial (the Constitution wasn't drafted until May 1787) went largely unnoticed by the fifty-two hundred alleged journalists who got chummed in.

My assignment for the *Miami Herald* was to attend what was billed as "the world's largest press party" and attempt to pay full price for everything. This proved almost impossible. For those whose employers forbade sponging, Disney cleverly had contrived a "guilt package" to take us off the hook. Price: $150 for a weekend that surely cost Team Rodent thousands per attendee.

I and several others politely declined the discount and asked to pay the same rates as regular tourists. After a lengthy negotiation, an exasperated desk clerk agreed to bill me the standard $190 a night for the hotel room. Later it was revealed that other journalists had allayed their professional consciences by paying as little as $35 for the same accommodations; one shitweasel actually took the room for $1. (If I had the name, I'd happily print it. To avoid embarrassing the offender, Disney declined to reveal his or her identity.)

The weekend was a wallow in temptation; everywhere we went, somebody was giving something away—and somebody in the press was glad to take it. The scene got so shameful that it turned funny. When Disney tour guides handed out free cowboy hats, a guy from a radio station snatched seven. When they offered free umbrellas, a woman writer scooted away with eleven. The Disney folks didn't seem annoyed or even surprised; they knew what kind of primitives they were dealing with. On the night of a big barbecue, Disney didn't even bother to put out cash registers. When three of us asked for a bill, our server laughed. We stacked $30 in cash on the table, but she wouldn't go near it. It was still there when we left.

Another afternoon, upon returning to my hotel room, I encountered a maid and a tall fellow in a blue blazer. They were delivering a Disney shopping bag loaded with munchies and gifts, including a "Shamu" doll. Shamu is the name of a trained killer whale at Sea World, a nearby tourist park not owned by Disney but included in the press-junket itinerary. I thanked my visitors but explained that I wasn't allowed to accept a free Shamu or a Mickey Mouse or anything else. They nodded pleasantly but made no move to take away the ditty bag. When I tried to hand it back, they stood Stepford-like, arms limp at their sides. "Please," I said firmly. The maid and the man in the blazer exchanged edgy glances. Finally they snatched up Shamu and departed.

To outsiders it must sound ridiculous, fussing over a few cheap souvenirs, but for journalists the principle is important. Disney's publicists don't invite people like us to the Magic Kingdom for the pleasure of our company. They're angling for positive press coverage, and that's usually what they get. For every snarky jab in the *Los Angeles Times* or the *Washington Post*, Disney enjoys miles of glowingly favorable column-inches in smaller hometown newspapers, which in the aggregate are read by far more Americans. It's true that most reporters can't be corrupted by a platter of spareribs, but the cumulative effect of Disney's indefatigable hospitality is a subtle seduction, an assiduously nurtured fondness. Arlene G. Peck, a newspaper columnist from Atlanta, insisted her reporting wouldn't go soft because of junket booty. Then she added: "What could you say bad about Disney anyway?"

That's another reason Team Rodent is able to devour the universe: The press is part of the team. And if you think we're easy in this country, you should see the packs of foreign journalists pigging out at the Disney trough. The rules are different overseas—in many places, no stigma whatsoever is attached to media junkets. The only limit to what gifts a reporter may accept is the capacity of his or her luggage.

My Disney press weekend—and the frayed dignity of the profession—was salvaged by one shining, spontaneous moment. We had been herded, all fifty-two hundred of us, into an auditorium, where we were told to expect a surprise guest. I believe Michael Eisner spoke first, followed by Justice Burger, who talked briefly about the Constitution. (Afterward Burger would say there was nothing inappropriate about combining a bicentennial tribute and a theme-park promotion, because Disney was well known as a "patriotic and history-minded enterprise.") To the jaded media in the auditorium, Burger intoned: "The Constitution is what we did with our independence."

Then he began to introduce the mystery guest. Quickly we figured out it was Nicholas Daniloff, the correspondent for *U.S. News and World Report* who days earlier had been released from a Soviet prison. Daniloff had been seized by the KGB on bogus charges of espionage, retaliation for the arrest of an alleged Russian spy in the United States. Daniloff's detention had been front-page news for two weeks, with Soviet authorities threatening a public trial. If convicted, he could have been sentenced to death. Finally Daniloff had been freed in a diplomatic swap for the accused Soviet spy.

The Disney gig would be the American reporter's first public reappearance on U.S. soil. It would take place before a large crowd of colleagues who considered him a genuine hero, and at a high-visibility event celebrating the heritage of liberty—for Disney, another masterstroke of PR.

But before Burger concluded the introduction, who should appear onstage behind him but Mickey Mouse. The saucer-eared idol stood there, jauntily swinging his overstuffed arms, waiting for the former chief justice to finish. To the reporter next to me I whispered: "Watch the Mouse! They're going to get the Mouse to hug Daniloff."

"No!" The reporter didn't believe even Disney would try such a stunt.

Yet that was precisely the plan: a fuzzy vermin hug for the returning political hostage—and a photograph. A photograph that would have run prominently in every newspaper in the free world: Mickey welcomes Nicky home from the Commie hoosegow!

We watched Team Rodent's choreography unfold with a mix of distaste and awe. Daniloff, pale and tired-looking, appeared in the wings. Sure enough, as soon as he strode onstage, the Mouse—that is to say, the person dressed up in the mouse outfit—wheeled with outstretched cotton arms . . .

And Daniloff, God bless him, deftly dodged the hug and breezed right past. Mickey was left grasping at ether. It was spectacular.

We gave our fellow journalist a hearty standing ovation, mostly for his grit in Moscow but also for his slick juke on the cartoon pest. Later a Disney spokesperson acknowledged that the company had been hoping for a photo of the two together. He said he saw nothing crass or demeaning in the idea, and I believe him. He truly didn't see it.

Jungle Book

APOLOGIES IN ADVANCE for the dead-rhinoceros story, but it must be told, mainly for what it says about my state of mind. Also, I've seen the pictures.

In the spring of 1998, over the protests of antizoo activists, Walt Disney World opened a theme park called Animal Kingdom. "From Dinos to Rhinos," promised the advance press release. "This newest and fourth major theme park at Walt Disney World Resorts sprawls across 500 acres reconfigured to look amazingly like animal reserves of Africa or Asia."

Typical Disney: Honey, I shrunk the Serengeti!

The new park offers the formulaic payload: fast-paced, telegenic, politically correct facsimiles of adventure. For instance, visitors are educated about threatened wildlife on a thrill ride called Countdown to Extinction. Meanwhile, a mock safari tracks ruthless elephant poachers through the bush.

But there's something different: "Celebrating man's enduring fascination with animals of all kinds, the new park provides natural habitats for more than 1,000 animals. . . . Rare and wonderful creatures, native to far-off lands, will include elephants, hippos, rhinos, antelope, lions, gorillas and much more, roaming freely. Natural barriers for safety are nearly invisible."

Incredible but true: Animal Kingdom is inhabited by real wild animals—not robots, not puppets, not holograms, not cartoons, but living and breathing creatures that (unless Disney starts tranking them) will eat, sleep, drool, defecate, regurgitate, sniff each other's crotches, lick their own balls, and occasionally even copulate in full view of the tourists. *Unprecedented* is the word for it. Never before has Nature been granted an assigned role in any Disney kingdom; up until now, a fiberglass crocodile was the dream Disney crocodile.

Control has been the signature ingredient of all the company's phenomenally successful theme parks; every thrill, every gasp, every delightful "surprise" was the product of clockwork orchestration. Once you paid your money and walked through the turnstiles, there was virtually no chance (until you walked out again) that anything unrehearsed would occur in your presence. "Nothing can possibly go wrong here, because nothing can possibly happen," wrote Elayne Rapping in a superb essay in *The Progressive*. "The idea that nature might be 'red in tooth and claw' was utterly foreign to [Walt] Disney's world view. But even more than blood, he abhorred dirt. Indeed, it is no accident that Disney's central ambassador is a neutered, hairless, civilized rodent—by nature the filthy scourge of every slum in the developed world."

Real vermin weren't the only animals shunned by Disney theme parks. In 1988 the Orlando resort was infested by a squadron of black buzzards that roosted indecorously atop the Contemporary Resort and other photogenic landmarks. The birds are large, stoop-necked, foul-smelling carrion eaters, and their glowering presence was deemed disruptive of the Disney ambience. In particular, the vultures were drawn to Discovery Island, one of the few locations in the Disney domain where wild native birds were welcomed.

And the buzzards came on strong. They vomited and pooped copiously, with no regard for the sensibilities of tourists. Equally dismaying were graphic reports that the buzzards were hassling the imported flamingos and preying on the helpless chicks of herons and egrets. Various methods were employed to frighten the aggressive raptors—flares, fireworks, helicopters—but the buzzards never left for long. Scores were captured and relocated far away, but it scarcely put a dent in the ever-growing Discovery Island flock.

Then, mysteriously, the birds began turning up dead. Accusations flew, and suddenly Disney—squeaky-clean Disney—found itself charged with shooting, starving, and even clubbing them with sticks. Sixteen state and federal wildlife violations were filed against Walt Disney World and several "cast members."

Black buzzards are protected by U.S. law and are thus allowed to go pretty much wherever they choose. As odious as they might be to humans, the birds play a crucial ecological role as scavengers. A murdered buzzard was rotten PR for any socially conscious multinational corporation. As Peter Gallagher wrote in *Tropic* magazine: "From the carcasses arose one of the messiest scandals in the 19-year history of Disney in Florida." Although the company disputed most of the animal cruelty charges, the ugly publicity didn't abate until Disney made peace with the Audubon Society and donated $75,000 to a trust fund managed by Florida's game commission.

To Disney executives, the buzzard incident soberly reinforced the idea that Nature is nothing but trouble. Wild creatures don't get with the program. They've got their own agenda.

Yet ten years later, here's Animal Kingdom. What made Disney change its mind about the zoo business? Money, of course. Tons of it was being made in central Florida by Busch Gardens, Sea World, and a host of not-so-slick competitors offering one attraction that Disney World didn't: live exotic critters. After a week at the Magic Kingdom, tourists of all ages yearn to see something with real fur. How many embraces from six-foot prancing chipmunks can a kid be expected to endure?

So Team Rodent made the bold move. It began, typically, by recruiting some of the top zoological experts in the country. Then it started shopping for wild animals. One of the first to be acquired was a rare black rhinoceros, a five-year-old female. Only three thousand of the animals are left in the world. Disney said it had purchased this one from a wild-game ranch in Texas. If all went as planned, the rhino would soon be released in a man-made African-style habitat, where it would be fed, watered, and protected for the rest of its life.

Again from the press kit: "Disney Imagineers have created tropical forests and jungles, streams and waterfalls, and savannas and rocky ridges— fascinating lands filled with natural beauty, where animals and visitors will participate in the unrehearsed dramas of life in the wild."

Unrehearsed—finally! No more remote-controlled crocs. Animal Kingdom would be the real deal, "unrehearsed dramas," meaning: If the critters decide to fight or fuck, we won't stop 'em.

Tragically, the young black rhinoceros never got a chance to test the limits of her Imagineered freedom. She died abruptly in the fall of 1997, months before the Disney zoo opened.

Discreetly the carcass was transported to the University of Florida in Gainesville, where a team of veterinarians performed a necropsy. It didn't take long to discover the cause of death, lodged deep in the animal's guts: a branchlike object, twenty-one inches long and three quarters of an inch in diameter. One end was sharp, having been cut with either a machete or a saw. The stick had punctured a lung and ignited a terrible infection. Disney's rhinoceros had died of pneumonia.

For doctors, the larger mystery was how the instrument of death had gotten inside the beast. Rhinos browse on grasses, leaves, twigs, and shrubs, and they're not always well-mannered eaters. It was conceivable that an exceptionally hungry animal could slurp down a twenty-one-inch branch without chewing it. And that would have been the working theory about Disney's dead black rhinoceros, that it had ingested the lethal stick from a pile of vegetation, cut for it as food by well-meaning handlers.

Except for one problem: The stick was found at the opposite end of the animal; specifically, in the last segment of the long intestine, within arm's reach of the rectum.

That strange and unsettling fact didn't fit the sloppy-eater scenario. A rhino's digestive tract is similar to that of a horse—twisting, lengthy, and convoluted. The doctors at the necropsy couldn't imagine how such a long sharp object could travel almost the entire circuit of a rhino's intestines before snagging. "Hard to believe," one of them stated flatly.

Yet the alternative seemed unthinkable: that a

person or persons unknown had savagely inserted the stick via another orifice. But who? Why? And, for God's sake, *how?* Although the Disney rhino had been known as exceptionally docile, it was mind-boggling to suppose she might have stood still long enough for . . .

Back and forth went the sensitive discussion, and ultimately the veterinarians chose the circumspect approach: They declined to make an official conclusion about how the branchlike object might have entered the mammal, or from which end.

However, the doctors did agree on one important finding: The nearly ossified condition of the intruder proved it had been inside the rhino's intestines *before* Disney had taken delivery of the animal. The news must have been a huge relief to company executives, providing a strong defense against accusations of neglect or cruelty. There'd be no need for a delicate inquiry as to who, if anyone, had so viciously violated the young pachyderm—whatever happened had taken place before the rhino arrived in Orlando. For added insurance, Disney botanists reclaimed the death stick and analyzed it. They reported that the tree it came from wasn't native to Florida.

Still, Team Rodent remained worried. No upbeat spin could be put on a story about an endangered creature expiring under mysterious circumstances on company property. With memories of the abused-buzzard fiasco still tender, a wall of secrecy went up. Anyone with knowledge of the rhino's demise was instructed to keep quiet, and to this day the attending veterinarians remain silent on the matter. Rumors about the rhino death have spread among employees throughout Disney's kingdoms; in one version the lethal instrument is said to be a two-by-four bristling with nails. A small story eventually did appear in the *Orlando Sentinel* and other newspapers, though with no mention of the possibility of foul play.

Upon learning how the rhinoceros had died, I assumed the worst: that the poor beast had been violated by a disgruntled or depraved Disney "cast member." It wasn't impossible. They had peepers and flashers, didn't they? Inside those stuffy costumes were real human beings with real human problems. What if Pooh had blown a gasket? What if Grumpy the Dwarf had no longer been able to suppress his darkest urges? Or maybe even one of the Mickeys? It was like something off the specialty video rack at Peep Land, this criminal debauchery of a rhinoceros; a rap verse off *The Great Milenko*. Sleaze lives!

Try to understand. For older, hard-core generations of Florida natives, no scandal is so delectable as a Disney scandal. This warped delight blooms out of deep resentment over the destruction of childhood haunts—an ongoing atrocity in which the Walt Disney Company remains gravely culpable, directly and indirectly.

Example: Peter Rummell, one the hotshots behind Celebration and the ill-fated Civil War theme park in Virginia, was hired away from Team Rodent in 1997 by the St. Joe Corp. Rummell's stated mission is to turn St. Joe, once primarily a paper manufacturer, into a leading developer of commercial and residential real estate. St. Joe happens to be the biggest private landowner in Florida, holding 1.1 million acres, much of it unspoiled. The potential for an environmental holocaust is enormous, and there's no comfort to be taken in the knowledge that a Disney spawn sits in command.

For those of us who grew up here, the anti-Mickey burn is chronic and ulcerating. It manifests in behavior that's not always mature, well reasoned, or even comprehensible to outsiders. As ghastly as the rhinoceros story is, I admit it perked me up a little at first. In my imagination I saw the

top-secret necropsy report landing with a slap
on Michael Eisner's desk; pictured his expression cloud as he scanned the shocking medical
description; watched the perspiration bead as he
contemplated the dreadful ramifications of an
endangered-mammal sodomization at a Disney
attraction. . . .

But no. Whatever happened to the poor beast
wasn't Team Rodent's doing. And yes, I was dis-
appointed at the news; crestfallen, if you want the
unflattering truth. A rhino scandal would have
been a dandy.

But why wish for such a perverse twist of
events? After all, aren't the folks at Disney mostly
good and decent and hardworking? And don't
they honor, in spades, their pledge to bring fun
and happiness to kids of all ages? Sure they do.
Being dutiful parents, my wife and I made several
pilgrimages to Walt Disney World when our
son was small, and he always seemed to have a
blast. How could such a mirth-giving enterprise
and the people behind it possibly be regarded as
evil? Even Insane Clown Michael—I know he's
not really a puppy-killing, rhino-molesting, foul-
mouthed ghostwriter of third-rate misogynist rap
songs. I know he's probably not even the Anti-
christ. He's just an exceptionally ambitious guy

trying to do a job, a guy who somehow has come to believe his own gushing press releases, a guy who honestly doesn't see the whole picture.

Maybe that's the kind of person it takes, and maybe that's what is so scary. To do what Eisner's Team Rodent does, and do it on that scale, requires a degree of order that doesn't exist in the natural world. Not all birds sing sweetly. Not all lakes are blue. Not all islands have sandy beaches.

But they can be fixed, and that is Disney's fiendish specialty. What Team Rodent has "re-created" in Orlando—from an African savannah to an Atlantic reef, from a Mexican pyramid to a Chinese temple—has been engineered to fit the popular image and to hold that charm for tourist cameras. Under the Eisner reign, nothing in the real world cannot be copied and refined in the name of entertainment, and no place is safe.

Chamber-of-commerce types in Key West got ticked off recently when Disney World unveiled its own quaint version of America's southernmost city, a half day's drive from the real thing. Granted, Disney's version of old Key West is cleaner, safer, and less margarita-sotted than the place after which it's modeled. Yet there's an element of insult—not to mention hard-hearted arrogance—in erecting a replica gingerbread town

to compete with the original for tourists. I don't
mind, because it means fewer rental cars speeding
past my house, but a business owner in Key West
might feel differently.

The point is, you can spend a solid month at
Disney World and never see evidence of the *real*
Florida, save for the occasional renegade buzzard
on a roadkill. The Magic Kingdom might as well
be in Tucson or Nashville or Tacoma; it wouldn't
matter. Once inside the gates, the experience
would be virtually identical—not at all unpleasant,
just fake. A sublime and unbreakable artificiality.
People might like it, but it's not natural.

Which brings us back to the story of Nala, the
lioness that escaped from the JungleLand zoo. For
three glorious days she eluded searchers who
tracked her by foot, 4-by-4, and helicopter. Satel-
lite trucks lined State Road 192 and concerned-
looking news correspondents beamed updates to
points around the globe. Was the lion heading
toward Disney World? How long before she got
there? Was it safe for tourists to stay? What should
they do if they encountered the animal? The
drama escalated hour by hour, experts warning
that the cat soon would be growing hungry. . . .

Now, in my lifetime I've seen many tourists so
poorly behaved they deserved to be eaten alive by

something. Tourons, they're called down here. They come to Florida, they trash the place, then they go. So out of reflex I began fantasizing what might happen if, by providence, a Disney touron crossed paths with the half-starved lion—a rustle in the vinyl topiary, a tawny flash, a muffled outcry . . . and somewhere the ghost of Charles Darwin exclaiming, "Right you are! This is what it's come to!" Or if not a loutish snowbird, then perhaps Ms. Kathie Lee Gifford, although for her the cat probably would need its claws. Another tasty possibility: Insane Clown Eisner himself, dragged down from behind as he hotfooted it across the phony savannah. Yo, Mikey, here's your frigging "animal kingdom."

But nothing so brutally ironic unfolded. Nala the lost lioness never made it to Walt Disney World; as a matter of fact, she headed in the other direction. Game wardens found her sulking beneath a palmetto bush, barely 150 yards from JungleLand. They zapped her with a tranquilizer dart and hauled her back to the cage, where she awoke and promptly began to chow down. The international press corps packed up and departed, as did the police, wildlife officers, and highway patrol.

And life goes on as before at the plastic

fantastic Reedy Creek Improvement District. All is safe. All is secure.

A new project, Disney's Wide World of Sports, has opened on what once was a two-hundred-acre wetland. Now there's a double-decker baseball stadium, an athletic field house, championship clay tennis courts, beach volley-ball (sixty miles from the nearest natural beach), and a parking lot for thirty-five hundred automobiles. Next to the ballfield an All-Star Cafe franchise is being completed, its investor-celebrities including Andre Agassi, Shaquille O'Neal, and Tiger Woods.

Touring the new sports complex with an Orlando reporter, Disney vice president Reggie Williams marveled, "I remember walking out here three years ago, months before we even began planning. There were snakes, spiders and all kinds of animals out here."

Reading that remark, I couldn't help but wonder about the water moccasins living in the marsh that Team Rodent had drained and bulldozed. And—God forgive me, it's nothing personal—I had a fleeting vision of young Agassi himself thrashing about on the red clay, a plump five-foot cottonmouth attached to his serving arm.

Reptiles are fond of cool, dark places, you see, and a Nike gym bag would do fine in a pinch.

"There were snakes, spiders and all kinds of animals out here."

But did Disney get them all? Did the bastards really get them all?

I don't think so.

ABOUT THE AUTHOR

CARL HIAASEN was born and raised in Florida, and his dream is to be banned forever from Disney World. He has worked for the *Miami Herald* since 1976 as an award-winning investigative reporter, magazine writer, and, for the last thirteen years, a metropolitan columnist. His novels include *Tourist Season*, *Native Tongue*, and, most recently, *Lucky You*, and have been translated into twenty-one languages. He has also contributed lyrics to two songs by Warren Zevon, "Rottweiler Blues" and "Seminole Bingo."

A Note on The Library of Contemporary Thought

This exciting new monthly series tackles today's most provocative, fascinating, and relevant issues, giving top opinion makers a forum to explore topics that matter urgently to themselves and their readers. Some will be think pieces. Some will be research oriented. Some will be journalistic in nature. The form is wide open, but the aim is the same: to say things that need saying.

**Look for these titles coming soon from
The Library of Contemporary Thought**

SEYMOUR M. HERSH
AGAINST ALL ENEMIES
Gulf War Syndrome: The War Between America's
Ailing Veterans and Their
Government

EDWIN SCHLOSSBERG
INTERACTIVE EXCELLENCE
Defining and Developing New Standards for the
Twenty-first Century

ANNA QUINDLEN
HOW READING CHANGED MY LIFE

KNOPF

From the best-selling author of *Strip Tease*

CARL HIAASEN

His funniest caper yet

LUCKY YOU

✳

Coast to Coast praise for *LUCKY YOU*

"The most entertaining novel I've read this year,
and the only one that made me laugh out loud."
——*Men's Journal*

"As funny and gritty as anything he's [ever]
written...LUCKY YOU pays off."——*Miami Herald*

✳

Hardcover • $24.00 • At stores everywhere
Also a Random House AudioBook and a Large Print edition

**Look for these wonderful novels
by Carl Hiaasen**

NATIVE TONGUE
"RIPS, ZIPS, HURTLES, KEEPING US
TURNING PAGES AT BREAKFINGER PACE."
—*The New York Times Book Review*

"RUTHLESSLY WICKED."
—*Atlanta Journal & Constitution*

SKIN TIGHT
"GOOD, MEAN FUN . . . A TWISTING, HIGH-
SPEED RIDE ON A ROLLER COASTER
WITHOUT BRAKES."
—*San Francisco Chronicle*

"A HIGH-SPEED TALE OF MURDER COVER-
UPS AND GONZO REVENGE . . . HIAASEN
DELIVERS EVERY TIME."
—*The Seattle Times*

**Published by The Ballantine Publishing Group.
Available wherever books are sold.**